TWINKLE, TWINKLE, LITTLE STAR,

and other bedtime lullabies

Twinkle, twinkle, little star -
How I wonder what you are!
Up above the world so high,
Like a diamond in the sky.
Twinkle, twinkle, little star -
How I wonder what you are!

Sleep baby sleep, and good night,
All the birds are asleep and out of sight,
Quiet the lambs on the hill,
Even the bumblebees are still.
Only the man in the moon
Is still nodding, but soon
Over him slumber will creep,
Sleep, baby, sleep, go to sleep.
Good night,
Good night.

Sleep, baby, sleep;
Thy father is watching the sheep,
Thy mother is shaking the dreamland tree,
And down falls a little dream on thee,
Sleep, baby, sleep,
Sleep, baby, sleep.

Sleep, baby, sleep;
The large stars are the sheep,
The little stars are the lambs, I guess,
And the bright moon is the shepherdess.
Sleep, baby, sleep,
Sleep, baby, sleep.

Hush-a-bye, baby, they're gone to milk,
Lady and milkmaid all in silk,
Lady goes softly, maid goes slow,
Round again, round again, round they go.

From breakfast on through all the day
At home among my friends I stay,
But every night I go abroad
Afar into the land of Nod.

All by myself I have to go,
With none to tell me what to do -
All alone beside the streams
And up the mountain-sides of dreams.

The strangest things are there for me,
Both things to eat and things to see,
And many frightening sights abroad
Till morning in the land of Nod.

A linden tree is standing
Beside a running stream;
I lay beneath its shadows
And dreamed a happy dream.

The rustling of its branches
Was like a lullaby;
I listened to its stories,
As I watched the clouds go by.

Matthew, Mark, Luke and John,
Bless the bed that I lie on.
Four corners to my bed,
Four angels round my head;
One to watch and one to pray
And two to bear my soul away.

Good night, God bless you,
Go to bed and undress you
Good night , sweet repose.
Half the bed and all the clothes.

I'll buy you a tartan bonnet,
And feathers to put upon it,
With a hush-a-bye and a lullaby,
Because you are so like your daddy.